My Family's Great Smoky Mountains Adventure

Written by:

Jeremiah J. Barnes

Photographs by:

James J. Barnes, Jeremiah J. Barnes, Jermaine J. Barnes & Shawnta S. Barnes

Brave Brothers Books
Indianapolis, Indiana

Brave Brothers Books LLC
1389 W. 86th Street #186
Indianapolis, IN 46260
www.bravebrothersbooks.com

My Family's Great Smoky Mountains Adventure

Copyright © 2018 by Jeremiah J. Barnes

Twitter@BraveBrosBook

All rights reserved. No part of this book may be used or reproduced by any means, graphic, electronic, or mechanical, including photocopying, recording, taping or by any information storage retrieval system without the written permission of the publisher except in the case of brief quotations embodied in articles and reviews.

The photographs included in this book were taken by the four members of the Barnes family: dad, Jermaine J. Barnes; mom, Shawnta S. Barnes, and children - Jeremiah J. Barnes and James J. Barnes.

Editors: Shawnta S. Barnes and Lisa Whrite
Cover & Interior Design: Suzanne Parada

Library of Congress Control Number: 2019942115

Published June 2019 in the United States by Brave Brothers Books LLC
ISBN 13: 978-1-7330242-9-7 (paperback)

DEDICATION

I thank my parents for taking me on this amazing trip.

I thank my family for believing I could write a book.

TABLE OF CONTENTS

CHAPTER 1 6

CHAPTER 2 9

CHAPTER 3 11

CHAPTER 4 18

CHAPTER 5 27

CHAPTER 6 32

About the Author 34

About the Photographers 35

CHAPTER 1

My parents said we were going to Gatlinburg, Tennessee during spring break. This is one place where you can see the Smoky Mountains. I had only seen mountains in pictures, and I was glad I would get to see them in person.

I was happy and a little nervous. My parents said we were going to stay in a cabin. There is a cabin on my school's property, but it doesn't even have a bathroom! I told my mom, "I don't want to use the bathroom outdoors." She chuckled and replied, "We are staying in a modern cabin. It will have bedrooms, a movie room, a game room, and a hot tub." Then, I got really excited!

Mom always takes a lot of pictures when we go on family trips. This time, I wanted to be a photographer too. I asked her if my twin brother James and I could have our own cameras to take with us.

Mom thought about it. She remembered she had boxes of old stuff she didn't use. Mom dug through a box of old cell phones, tablets, and random cords. She found two digital cameras in there, showed us how to use them, and let us practice at home before the trip.

Mom showing me how to use the camera.

I took photographs of my pet bearded dragon Zippy, the fridge, a photo of my parents, my Lego guy, and Mom. I don't think Mom was happy to be photographed. A few days later, it was time to go on our trip.

CHAPTER 2

Mom gave us a list and said, "Follow this list, so you don't forget anything." After we packed our stuff, we drove to a vehicle rental store to get another SUV. I'm not sure why. Both my parents have SUVs. Mom drove hers back to the house, and Dad followed in the rental. James and I kept looking out the back window of Mom's SUV to wave at Dad.

Once we got home, we put our bags into the rental SUV. Mom had another list. It was the schedule. "Jermaine, we are behind schedule," she said to Dad. He frowned, and Mom looked frustrated.

Dad drove out of Indiana to Ohio. Next, he drove through Ohio to Kentucky. After driving out of Kentucky, we were finally in Tennessee.

It was dark once we arrived in Tennessee. We didn't leave when Mom wanted, and Dad did not like driving in the dark. Mom said, "We should have left on time." Dad said nothing. He was trying to find the cabin office in the dark. We stopped there to get the keys to the cabin. Then, Dad drove past different buildings, people, and a dog. After getting a little lost, we finally found the cabin.

The cabin was awesome. I walked around with my brother. We looked at the hot tub and the bedrooms. I asked him, "Do you want the room on the top floor to be ours?"

"Yes!" He replied.

Mom had a hard time taking our photo because we kept jumping around during the game.

Then, we went downstairs to see the movie room. Next, we played air hockey in the game room.

We went back upstairs and checked out our room some more. I wanted to watch *DuckTales*, but Dad let my brother choose. He chose *Tom and Jerry*. It was hilarious. We laughed a lot. After watching, we fell asleep.

CHAPTER 3

The next day, Mom and Dad woke us up and said it was time to explore.

We got lost again, and Mom was frustrated again. Dad was not listening to her directions.

Mom came to see what was taking James and me so long to get ready. James took her picture, and I don't think she liked that.

After driving to Gatlinburg from our cabin, we had to find a place to park. The parking machine was having problems and wasn't taking payments from credit or debit cards. A lot of adults looked mad, and Dad was one of them. He did not have cash. James and I had money. We had our birthday party a month before the trip, and Mom and Dad said we could bring our money to buy stuff. Dad came back to the SUV and said, "Let me have your birthday money bag." Then, he took some of our cash! My brother crossed his arms and said, "No fair!" Dad replied, "Life is not fair."

Next, we walked to get some lunch. Mom and Dad had been to Gatlinburg before, and they really wanted to eat at a place they liked called Bubba Gump Shrimp Company Restaurant and Market. I thought the name was weird, but most of the food I ate was good. My brother thought so too. We both had a hamburger, French fries, and jello. I had never eaten jello, and I didn't like it.

I looked outside while waiting for my food.

James colored a picture of a shrimp while he waited.

After lunch, we went to the Ripley Aquarium of the Smokies. My brother and I love aquariums! We saw lots of cool animals, and we took photographs of them. We even took pictures of each other to have proof that we were there.

My brother and I had so much fun taking pictures.

I tried to get a picture of Dad and the shark, but they would not stay still.

James tried to take a picture of Mom and Dad. He also had problems getting Dad in the picture.

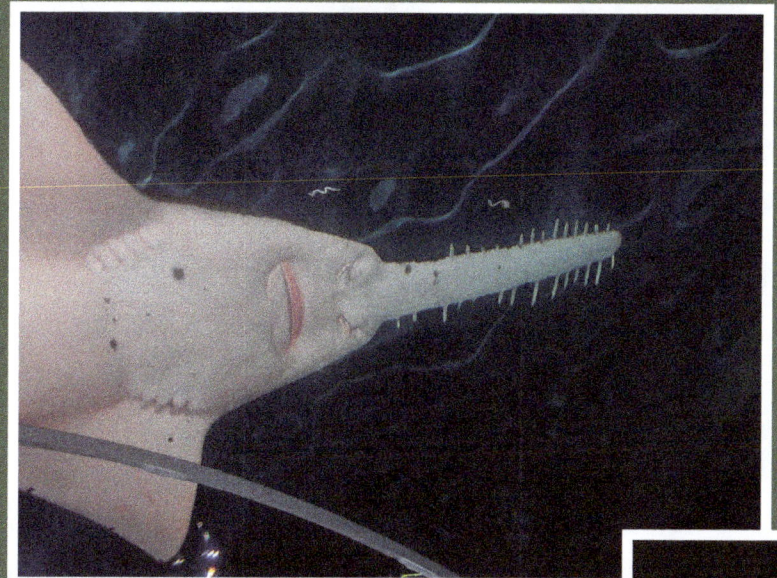

This is a carpenter shark. People also call it a sawfish since its nose looks like a saw.

These are horseshoe crabs.

This is a seahorse.

15

This is a Japanese Spider Crab.

I took a photo of James in front of some jellyfish.

Then, James took a photo of me.

After we left the aquarium, we rode a ride called Earthquake. We got on the ride, and we buckled our seatbelts. I was happy, but my brother seemed nervous. He wouldn't sit still and kept looking around. I told him, "This isn't real; it's just a ride." He replied, "I know, and I'm not scared!" Things looked like they were falling on this ride. As the ride continued, he laughed with me at the fake earthquake. Then, the ride got us. We both jumped when a big gorilla popped out and surprised us.

I thought we were going to do something else, but Mom and Dad said they were tired. They were ready to drive back to the cabin. James and I were full of energy.

James and I had fun in the hot tub. I'm wearing the green and black swimsuit.

After returning to the cabin, I asked Mom, "Can we go inside the hot tub?" She said, "Yes." Mom, Dad, my brother, and I got in. The water was nice and warm. I had a lot of fun. My brother and I took turns holding our breath under the water. We challenged each other to see who could hold his breath the longest, and I won each round. I felt so good because the last time we did this challenge in a pool, James kept winning. This was the first time I ever won.

CHAPTER 4

The next day, we went to see the Smoky Mountains. Mom really wanted to get a picture by the sign that said, 'Smoky Mountains,' but it was too crowded for Dad to find a place to park. Instead, we went to another place that was good for taking pictures.

James likes to act goofy in photos. He kept making weird faces. Dad would take some photos, and Mom would look at them and shake her head. After a few times of this, Mom gave up. She told James, "I guess you'll just look crazy in the pictures." I don't think James cared.

After taking pictures, Dad drove into the Great Smoky Mountains National Park. We walked around and saw the Smoky Mountains. We also saw a waterfall, and we took some more pictures. A nice man offered to take a family photo of us. James even tried to look normal in the picture.

Check out my brother's silly face!

My brother and I were happy to see Cataract Falls.

We took a family photo. James did not make a weird face, and Mom was happy!

I also saw a cool tree. I went inside and had Mom take a photo of me.

This would be a great place to read a book.

Later, we were able to walk on the Appalachian Trail.

My brother and I are standing next to the Appalachian Trail sign.
I bet you can guess which one of us is James.

We also took some photos on the trail. The trail was muddy. We walked for a while then turned around and walked back.

We wanted to run on the trail. "Do you want to slip and fall down the mountain?" Mom asked.

James has a serious face in this picture.

After we finished walking on the trail, we stood on the Tennessee and North Carolina state line.

This was my first time standing on a state line.

Next, we went to MagiQuest. MagiQuest is a place where you get to complete quests. It was our first time, so we had to go to a room to learn how to play the game. After the training, we went upstairs and completed a quest. Once we were done with one quest, we did another.

My favorite part was using the wand during the quests.

I wanted to do a third quest, but everyone was hungry. Dad drove to a restaurant that had sandwiches and soup. James took a photo of me with Mom and Dad.

Dad is tall. It is easier to take his photo when he is sitting down.

CHAPTER 5

We decided to spend most of the day at the cabin during our last full day in Tennessee. The tub in our room made bubbles like the hot tub, and Mom put bubble bath in the tub. We had fun covering ourselves with bubbles.

This was the best bubble bath ever!

Later, I got hurt. I cut the back of my foot. I was swinging it up high, and it came down on the air hockey table. I asked Dad to help me. He cleaned the blood off, and Mom gently put my sock on after wrapping my foot with a paper towel. Dad said sternly, "Everyone needs to sit down. We don't need anyone else getting hurt." He put the movie *Coco* in the DVD player to keep us on the couch.

Next, we went to the store to buy a proper bandage for my foot. After that, we went to the Guinness World Records Adventure. There were challenges you could do there. I thought a lot of the challenges were hard. Then, I found one I thought I could do. You had to look at a diagram and build a house. I didn't have enough pieces, so I yelled out, "I quit!" Mom turned to me and said, "You can use my pieces." I decided to try again. I didn't think I could do it, but I did.

The Rubik's Cube challenge was hard.

I almost gave up. I am glad I kept trying.

Last, we went to Ripley's Marvelous Mirror Maze. They gave us glasses and plastic gloves to wear inside the maze. I had a hard time keeping the gloves on my hands, and the mirrors in the maze made our bodies look funny.

The maze was connected to a candy store. We used some of our birthday money to buy some candy, and Mom and Dad took a piece from each of our bags. James said, "No fair!" Mom replied, "This piece of candy is mine because of the parent tax."

CHAPTER 6

The next morning, I was a bit sad. It was our last day in Gatlinburg, Tennessee. I was having so much fun; I was not ready to go home.

For breakfast, we went to Flapjack's Pancake Cabin. I got a teddy bear pancake. They used big and little pancakes to make a bear. The waitress gave me syrup to pour on my pancakes. The pancakes were delicious, and I ate them all.

After breakfast, we went back to the cabin to pack up and leave. Mom said, "Make sure you use the packing list." Mom and Dad walked around the cabin to make sure we did not forget anything.

Dad put our bags into the SUV and told us to buckle our seatbelts. When Dad drove past MagiQuest, I took one last photo with my camera of the building. There were so many places we did not have time to visit. I hope I can go back to Gatlinburg again soon.

About the Author

Jeremiah J. Barnes is an eight-year-old second grader who lives in Indianapolis, Indiana. His best friend is his identical twin brother, James. In his spare time, he likes to read scary stories, mysteries, and graphic novels, write stories, play soccer, play games on his Chromebook, and attend Indiana Pacers basketball games.

About the Photographers

Jermaine J. Barnes is a senior Oracle database administrator. In his spare time, he enjoys playing basketball, sports with his children, and video games. He also enjoys watching action and science fiction movies and anime.

Shawnta S. Barnes is an educator and education writer. In her spare time, she enjoys reading, writing, and growing food.

Jeremiah J. Barnes and **James J. Barnes** are identical twins who enjoy playing sports with their dad and gardening with their mom. They love to eat pizza, tacos, and Brussels sprouts. In their spare time, Jeremiah loves watching cartoons on Netflix, while James loves writing and illustrating graphic novels.

www.ingramcontent.com/pod-product-compliance
Lightning Source LLC
Chambersburg PA
CBHW060856090426
42736CB00025B/3496